I Love It Though

I Love It Though   Alli Warren

Nightboat Books
New York

ISBN 978-1-937658-60-1

Design and typesetting by Margaret Tedesco
Text set in Trade Gothic and Book Antiqua

Cover art, Suzie Brister: *Hi-Lo Rabbit on Country Road*, 2013
Archival pigment print on Hahnemuhle photo rag, 32 x 32 inches
Courtesy of the artist

Cataloging-in-publication data is available
from the Library of Congress

Distributed by University Press of New England
One Court Street
Lebanon, NH 03766
www.upne.com

Nightboat Books
New York
www.nightboat.org

Table of Contents

A Yielding Hole For Light

Where were you when the West
Antarctic Ice Sheet began to collapse?
On the way to Iowa City
to see my first sumac and coming
to know its name in asking
it's the way of coming to know
as if in revelation instead of simple clarity
I tell BB what I want around me
are the ripe and tender ones
wine the color of weather
the lush bearing of our longing
going on in my way, stupidly sincere
one foot in the office the other lolling
about the field, do you prefer the gravel
to the scrub grass? I prefer the ear
to the throat, calling choice
what's ancient, trained
to chew on the cork like it was mine to do with

I'm not necessarily not destroyed
by the loon looming on the horizon
you accuse of having no inside
I stand under persimmon and see Frank

and the white bowl, heat machine
beaming luxuriously, ground of everything
ground of light, makes the field wider,
makes hedges fall
Or the courage or not
of me and my friends
orbital in lilt, directive in drink
while container ships brim
and caps and bergs
slope across the slog
I want to be able to continue
to love to stay alive
The epigraph belongs to Gloria Gaynor
the green pervades, it's a diamond, we all are

Lunchtime with Woodwinds

I wish I could write a song
to make the world
yield to this rushing

lapping what starts
tonguing what parts
any possible other world than this

inertia for pink medallion
inertia for those skeptics
in the building

who think of the unknown
as hemorrhage — quick stop
that thing from surfacing

I want to rub along
the webbing I want nothing but
the cove's yawning jaw

for how else could possibility emerge
you see that honey
seeping through cracks?

let's consider unbearable facts
beat this meat against the rocks

you call that virtue? knock knock

is this the proper place for the symposium?
small of my back requests unfolding
requests enveloping entry

call the operators
to open pathways
to vessels which gleam

rightly and rush
to make this here inlet
a humid blue bowl

to resist enclosure
and the loaded laying down
of structure on soft earth

as desire can never perish
blind in the rush of weeds
trying to get a glimpse

of the law
falling away
and in passing breathing lift

Out on the Wire

If I dip the tip
between the old world
and the same
river twice
how to measure
the wind at my back
who harks here
against misery against
private diminishment
attachments precede us
and we are obliged
to replicate conditions
on the compound
They hoot for work and cart
in flesh & commerce
we want the morning
of unstructured grace
parted lips & northern lights
to harness the force
of a thousand layings on
a gaping mouth
of no market purpose
walking blind

out into the road
toward the end
of this world-system
or is that just
local lore?
I lug this bucket around
for tillage and for trade
it's what I use
to feed the wolf her milk

The Last Great Heteronormative Hope

On the way to the bar
I pass three other bars

What bodies accomplish
as bodies alone

The repeated insistence
of certain affects

the wetness of a girl
on the phone fingering taut cord

as seen on drunk with dreams
a coveted bloom of indecision
dots the horizon

I toe the light
I jab my finger in the peephole
nay, I ginger gently

sniffing the clear-cut future
and dangling before the nose
the tenor of a clinching gift

as seen in fidelity to our newest member
self-propagating aeroelastic dream fluff

Whose heartland
whose gray beast?

In cahoots with associations
in conjunction with constitutive credit

I heard you say cheap trick
I heard you say charmed life

Those fixed and eternal things
face of the whole
hammerhead cock

in the same possible world
in which I txt my boss

and scrawl anti-state messages
on my eyeblack

A Date with the Cages

As ships start
from their tunnels
yanking half-held tongues
and dangerous pronouns
the moon isn't it suddenly there
blinking in the airy application
of rights and uses

I lift a few through the net
and break a sweat
I hit the showers
and bang my head
against the closed-cell
extruded polystyrene foam
shaft at the heart
milk in the big absent

At the very moment of my possible
future heroic active aiming
Chris says life is long
I trip on a log and go under
cover I bury my face in
that warm crevice

the eye of which is bigger
than a human head how
wherefrom we've come
swallows the sea deep
constellates tomorrow

If you can't win
with the one you love
love the inflated object?

At the center of the mass
in the scar of my ear
is metal more than
you've ever seen
once it touches air
every cop goes poof

There's Always Some Bird Dog

Guards demand we waltz
the teeming hedge
soldiers spread
but can't quell
what wells

worthwhile's a made shape
wafting about
in the night so green
all bright ornament
and creamy delay

I take off my hat
I get off and walk

O skin be strong
don't end at lending
nouns to property

consult the ear
consult the air

claim common right
to lap the excess
as a lock's for frisking
a gale's gaping gate

They say the submarine
which waves no flag
is a violator vessel

how soft its coax
how smooth its thick white head

adorned and anointed
the bodies of my loves

the fear grins
of great apes

Just My Imagination

the black forest sings

in little bursts

in hums and cleaves

a fictive future

I guide my hand through

an absurd and sticky

habit whose force

an inflatable estate

along the lobate plains

I flop along the line

and thumb the brink

out in the clearing

beneath the beach

the best dreams are those

that fail most comprehensively

women and children

build the barricades

Protect Me From What I Want

I did it for the data I did it for the lulz

I did it for the money I did it for the children

I did it for the health of the chickens

I did it to overturn attrition I did it to retake the city

I did it for the up-goats for the good company for the habit of

my pleasure & the unknown links in sub-domains

I did it so that everyone would gasp

I did it for the glory I did it for the potential of psychic space

I did it for the lithe production I did it for the team

I did it for the nation to animate paralysis to get numb with

consensual promise

I did it for the people their disambiguation their predatory

lending

I did it to carry my propriety into property

I did it for the things that resonate around me

I did it for archaic loss I did it for the clustering

I did it for the rope chain I did it for the manny

I did it for the decimals I did it for the sake of my name my
     privilege my primary wives
I did it for the thousands of unknown civilians I did it for the
     sense of self-pride I did it for the lush submerging
I did it for the universe it amused me
I did it for the music I did it for Foxconn
I did it for the photos I did it for the booty I did it for the
     dithering I did it for the reorgs
I did it for the love of cash your honor
I did it for the welfare of my box
I did it for the workings of the inner ear I did it to return to
     camp refreshed
I did it for the emerging world I did it for the people at work
I did it for the systematic recourse to subcontracting
I did it to dispense with all obstacles to profit
I did it for the enduring light
I did it to learn my handicraft in the daytime

I did it for the freebies I did it for the chicks

I did it for the cycle of escalation for the unbound acts I did it
for the surprise of what might be in them

I did it for the betterment of the brotherhood I did it for the
pauperization of the population

I did it for the norms for the basis of the degree I did it to not
look back wistfully

I did it for the woman I loved I did it for the greatest
country the world has ever known I did it for their
flourishing

I did it for the same reason as you
for the free-play of my bodily and mental activity
for the pleasure of my friends

I did it for the moonshine I did it for the endorphins

I did it for the districts to the north for the public at large

I did it for the portable hoard

I did for the spreading pleasure I did it for the eager fatback

I did it for the idea of the middle class

I did it for the free beer in Montana I did it for the vital rice crop

I did it for the motherland for the halibut for the great Nile

   abounding I did it for the love of blogging

I did it for the present tenses I did it for the herd

I did it for the chicken heads I did it for the butter cream

I did it for the government of property I did it for the unloved

   and unknown

I did it for the terror of the totally plausible future

I did it for the function of the mass of agricultural serfs

I did it for thieves rogues and striking workers I did it to fully

   exploit any sale potential

I did it for the sheer fact of my feelings for the buoyancy of

   your touch

I did it for the entire sweater

Mercy

It's not that I own a Lambo
or even that I am sitting in one
but being called as I am
thirsty or chicken-headed
when the sum of my desire
directs me to sit and watch
the blue flag breeze
in company, in "hurt and thrill"
chamomile, pâté, cherries, and champagne
sounds so luxurious when you lift your pointer
slowly like that, and it is, I do
in the sticky groove of restless longing
but no one's heroic in humidity
no one's heroic with scrambled eggs on toast to eat
and soup of pureed watercress to eat

I point to the back of my skull or Lily
of the Nile, and on my collarbone?
the sun I think will heal everything
or Elaine's peach pooling on the big brick floor
I want to open to remain coming lush adaptive ode I want
to arrange abreast along the marking underbrush and make refrain
to be lifted again by the underarms and brought out into the rain

but one gape follows the next
and the story slinks to meet its instinct
where wingtips merge into priority
with permission and with violence
are they pointing at the stubble or am I a hen
watery because I've not entirely chosen
being driven through a hill from both directions
swollen beyond season, bleeding from the beak

Salt Lakes & Sand Dunes

My wife was dead
My wife had died
It comes in rushes
as through a trunk
not that I know anything, anything
in the dark of preposition's promise
in jeggings and a button up
I send out a call
on account of other causes
unknown or unsaid
with my yawp up
against guilt and dearth
without foreknowledge
without regret
My pathetic life in shrimps
doling out tincture
in the troubled territories
The wisest person I know — the ocean
regurgitated all and turned back
to the one who came wielding it
Bayed at what
I thought was the moon

Blue as the news
crisis of kairos
and bold rocky fact
I came here in relief to expect myself
in the cold out tonight
under BofA
lolling on the sod spent

Tunics, Trousers, and Cloaks

I sing of something that cannot speak its name

though its signature is everywhere

Of sentimental feeling

and immaculate behavior

Of pre-pledged consent

to the national future

in the tumult of the folds

I make a hole

for glory wherever

In alehouses and down laneways

in gross profusion

and self-pollution

Whence the sucking commences

it lives more the more it sucks

All the evil things of the world will have full sway

To get dressed

I need the help of a trained hand

The Tower of Winds

on ascending the pitch

in order to surprise her

with a water clock

and a wind vane

in order to return to the states

to enjoy patrimony

in the sputter and heat

I wet the pellet in my neb

and curse my horses

along the reeking bank

and of all the gifts I sing

intent for intent

with garlands & candelabras

with laurel branches & ox-heads

not even worth my weight in hops

and you all in your laughing

rolling in togas in the aisles

Index of Social Membership

Foolhardy with no ice on patriots' day
comrades gone to fetch the hog
pressed the blade wrist-ward
and came back intact
by which I mean flayed
from waist to waist
left for living dead
loft-deep in glass
Rocks call out your facts
Out with the minions!
Raise your disemboweled hands!

Who here daily distends
having had a feeling
in the bush-deep
you've got some uh
you've got a bit of blood
pooled at the opening
Here let me mark the place
where the deed was done
and the clock stopped or shot
went reeling in the night down

gentrified avenues & littered laneways
stricken in the flank
surely as sirens sound
Faith ain't nothing
but weakness & credit
Miss it terribly need a little dog

The National Future

In the courtroom
as in the market
the foundation reeks
along an endless
intergenerational chain
of patriarchal provision

To reintegrate the runaways
orators and their orations
blame "lower lust
and mere meat"

by which they mean their modernity
upon which rests
the whole noxious system
of price over promise

In the gathering place
in the meat of possibility
I wave a flag for brute feeling

I daily pay court
and consort in taverns

sucking heartily on the teats
and profiting off the gaunt
carnal mess

In sowing season?
sulfur, tar, and torches

Split Apart and Plummet Down

crisis from the first
and in death mask went
mark-making through the ether
stepping over the dead
in the avenues and territories
the polished Nikes
of my compadres
hack the tap
until it loses value
and the pen breaks
in strategic use
by power in all its
minor forms
with money in the prisons
to make people believe
in keeping going
takes precedence
over joy
in the dream I asked
are you happy
when the fish diminish

Take Care of Yourself and Get Plenty of Rest

Steeped in the cooing surround
unmoved in the threshold
stalking that entrance stockings
stained compelling every thing
to cling to clump
as is our wont

As if sympathy with one
were support for the other
I move among loves
as aims that animate
the lack of which holds me

or anything a mouth has to utter
panting on the sofa
kicking up the ice
lilting wilting middle
where an outside used to be

When I said I was going
to the bar I meant
no death, no death
free the big fish

holed up in pens
some imp of a candle's
no light, there's blood in the silt
I forage & fold & go all frond
clinging as much in cause
as consequence
in the crowded den
of your heart's stadium

I gather reams
and kettle the coho
I lurch where
I should listen
Only the mercury is true

Palpating the Scar

brimming at the limit oozing

hole where the heart should be

all the usual palliatives

until they no longer suffer

the musk of indecision

if only by virtue

of vowing to be

fungible that whole

biorhythm thing

as long as it rings

could a polity

would a

I like the look of light

on moss its rank

inability to oath

those who persist

in entering breach

No Good Habits

With a mouthful of muddy wallboard
in the afternoon's eclipse of opportunity
I join an armless band of side-saddlers
making overtures during flush times
to the night heron on the super blue
we fail to hold true to
Drawing out the vowels
trading paint at the bend
okay it's only 7:30
but the nascent wing of your breath
on my ankles squawking
under lid of what children I won't have
and in that mirror
shirtless, but on my face?

Flogged against the fence
caved in the hull
an embarrassment to all
decency they'll clap your arm off
and call it self-determined
auto-avoidance as if the disappeared
still scrawl mourning songs
with what gig and agog

I could begin to find
playing lollipop with a nightstick unrewarding
"No one even cares in the outer metros"
I want to be absolved of regrets and relieved of nostalgia
The new more humane tank is 20 x 30 ft.
The earth and the sky are one fist

Total Vocation

If I press my upper territories
against another dream
to coat the loss of merging
is desire a thick set band
so tight about the jaw that it breaks
the belt and the jaw both

If I tug up from under
fluttering attachment
reduce drift and perfect alignment
is there any space left in the breathing world
within site of that sweat beading
on the right side of your open neck
with pants so tight everyone
will understand the conditions that produced them

The connection will hold, or it will not
There is copper and industry
for the structure to take
or there is not
Where the lap and where the head dunked in brine
where the tease of a toe dipped in a tub deferred

Is this not refreshment or refinement
or the flecked soup of what won't be

I linger in that residue
uninitiated and dumb in repetition
"employing all my strength to be resigned"
My landlady paints the whole thing forest green
the beak, the hole, and the emotional austerity
which precedes and surrounds it

O malleable heart
O irreducible cement
I am left-footed in deliberation
in domination's lusty grip
clamoring for enlargement of the spheres
The indication on the outside
represents the tokens on the inside
Sound only exists as it is going out of existence

Something is Coming Toward Us

Flaunting in the atrium, ostentatious at the gates
I saw a shooting star thru a window on Alcatraz Ave
& cladding struck up against those who demand
We stomach the stick and tend the commode
They're selling trees in the paint store! trees in the paint store
Datebook chips in the soft skin of our wrists
On NBC, CNN, and NPR broken windows are weeping
We'll have 35 apples and shrieking in the thickets
Aloft in the air golden and golden the dial among the mounds
So much is stunted in understanding of what a light can be
They storm the scrimmage line and clear-cut bran and germ
We want the petal unto itself, the unalterable vessel
The arc end of the precipice grows 1.9% annually
What was popular music like before the crisis?

The Women Perform Their Ablutions

After the end of the world
I go to wash your clothes in the Arno

Extension in the bright world
nothing, nothing, nothing
and stars

What but faith
can breach the void?

Friendship, empathetic
yawning, watching two crows
as a group of boys
venture out into the stop & frisk

If I give skin a syntax
or touch the swallow as it lifts
that a finger might slip

If lush indicants
attuned, throbbing, burst

Where is the net which saves
rather than traps
why is there something not

Let love run the radios
baby baby please don't go

On the Levelers Everyday

Clawing at the new world
from the cattle car
savoring the slow ache
of inflexible need
with some bit of skull
stuck to my peep-toe platform wedges

The sound of that shore slapping
coaxes me I like to look upon the waters
and call them green and call them
the disaster of compulsory exchange

I dip my snout in the opening
slot where a coin tarries
to raise flag for common property
I mean the end of profit
the clerk, the apparatus
of good functioning
Where nomads love
and build no hedges
So the window disappears
or someone opens it

Dear causal moment
dear inflated object
Who can live, who gets to eat
what's a sidewalk, what's a street
Let's loot the establishments
I mean feed each other

Can anyone identify this flower?
the bell's about an inch thick

Everybody Loves A Runt

The morning after
on the couch of what would being
an agent feel like
I'm talking to my shoe

Where is that balcony
beaming skyward
what do my lungs do
and my liver
on this earth

If in my ear
there is a choir
I am not alone
and lifted by that number
into the temperate air
where bulbs like buds be strung

I cave my breath and back
over the bar's amber pleather
and make a knot
over the dull closure
of safe-keeping

Flowering cacti
generous middle
if eating is aim-inhibited kissing
perversion is a turning
away from the earth

I want curiosity
over consolation
fantasies of function and
I've got legs
in the pointless humidity
of a Thursday morning

Slantwise on the Skyline

I make a list of demands
the right not to be
always a sight
distant splendor of night
baying at the foyer

On holydays I stew
in bed as long as possible
and lay equal claim
to each axiom

to fill this hole
with bottom earth
with cedar, cypress, yucca, and yew

I want to be sucked up into the air and released
without any raiment or kirtle
with strings in accord
with what exceeds us

Praise be to Venus, to waxy embrace
How many halves have you?
count the bridges that cross the bay

The Finest Vellum You've Never Seen

with my boss's

boss's boss

in greatest agitation

and frost on the nightshades

I like to fetch

the hereinafter

swerving on this

pill I took

watching water

break back

against the land

to lift a spell

off the tongue

to free gales

turbines lease

and landlords loan

to collect what lodges

in the crevice

of a possible

necking this draft of what

sings and stands

each time

we mount the fold

Parades Go By

Raise your hand if
you've seen them
running in the field
without cleats

to launch a fleet
into the cold arms
of the sea at the mouth
of functionality

in the air above the sky
quarantined I watch
where ships set out
from this enclosure

to become pliant
in self-enjoyment
with all the others
to hold her limp neck

where a wet hand
can never know
or the simplest thing
and swallowing

A Better Way to Zone

Habits accrue
in circular pattern
and living occasion
swollen among what
the dead have to teach us

So, ear, be an instrument for thought
Tide, bring some
little green thing to dust
behind my eyes

Touch the hotpoint
and drag the tongue
over the fat belly
of a flapping fish

Sticker book
of farm animals
Sticker book of ole timey cats
What is life and how shall it be governed?

With blind devotion
and endurance in the impossible

for guts in everything for roots
in plain sight

Share a lung
Accumulate none
Say hello to the crow

There are certain chord progressions
one should avoid

The Most Oral of Animals

I like to smear
the balmy heretofore
across my arms
and graze in the heat
of what unfurls

I mean I'm bound
by that song
baying at the rim
Coming day come
alight and mounting

Gills go under sea
loot the larder
wrench the built form

Voice be a crowd
make honey from stone
sap from stubborn trunk

Two in the top
of the market

one in the abundant
assembly of givens

Bulbous at the base
pungent in the plank
rum buns in every port

To the Fledglings

I could clean this shovel

     or nap in its possible use

I could mend the clasp and the seam

I could make lace, iron, and houses

I could plead for more work

     & merge onto the pedestrian highway, working a fast-acting sud into the pallet of exhaustion while pigs on high horseback pen and prod

     or I could demand the leisure to make love and laugh

     as the honeydew and grapefruit, wisteria brine and datura liquor, as this relentless mortal earth

I could wash the grass

I could raise the mainsail and frame the wind

I could count on bosses to promulgate the mandate that life on earth is for suffering

I could defend like a philosophical drone the legalistic
  ease of uninterrupted aesthetic progress

      or I could bounce a brick ball off the face of what keeps us
      from just sustenance

      & reach a gloved hand through tempered shards to get at
      the bounty

I could evict the germ and the bran

I could pay off the last of what it took to confirm the lump is
  mobile but not for now malicious

I could extract my milk teeth

      or develop a diet of only snails and champagne

I won't flatter commerce and its confidants

I won't seal the hatches and make a steambath of the precinct

      I'll build a coat of sweat from fucking and foraging, for
      the sensation of their twinning

      I want to rest in the self-same place where my fellows
      strike a bunt against the night

I could cultivate a work-centered identity

I could ban blood, cake, air, ooze, ease, loaves

I could sleep in this spittoon or call a bodice a blanket

     or lazily graze on the horizon wherefrom a perpendicular
     love will knock the bow of my self-sustained boat

     the way borders burst open under their propensity for
     feasting

I could be a revitalized basin, I could be steel upturning the earth

I could be ashamed of bedding the inedible fruits of flowering
   plants, or for occupying a dwelling in which there is a bed or a
   window or a having at all

     or I could be a water rat self-scratching my flank gland,
     lining the palace walls with sweetest fecal syrup

I want to be in the lazing camp surrounded by unirrigated wilding

     aligned with alliterative pattern and inordinate demand

     confounding the anthropologist and the academic

So while I could be an accomplice to the flood

>or insist on property as my right to white life

>or saunter out into the surf of the street with the gaze and the beard and the bread and the get called genius and heir

>better to ladle in the brothy endurance of subsistence and resistance

If I mimic the pit's angle of repose and catch the downward flow in my yawning yawp

>will I exceed containment

>will I be a scandal to productive logic

>or a pencil palm waving in grayest coming storm

I could pile the pantry onto the 3rd rail and braise all day by power of perspiration

I could truck with the teat of national interest and competitive eating

I could call the sap-extracting club my unwavering god

> or I could be a gainfully unemployed brow on a grassy
> pillow

> orienting giving to the generous pyracantha of bright red
> globes

I could slurp this soursoup

I could enumerate lessons learned and forks swerved from

I could be restraint, perfected hailing, efficient breeding

> but the breadth I want is napping, phototactic

> bathing in the drowsy milk of dewing over doing happened
> upon like the push-up cacti me and my love saw sprung at
> the lake

Nature never made no merchant

Sabotage is sister to system, that's what eating is, that self
    same momentum

Give me bumpers of burgundy and the purring whir of jasmine

I want to negate productivity on my back, in this clover

softest heels never near pounding the atriums of tribute

As bread is 90% air, may breathing be largely bread, and so too
endeavoring, forever sated

Andromeda Has Fine Recompense

& I ate an egg unannounced
drunk on that breed, rug
burned, trying to convert
infernal alternatives
to the star we want to thrive
down in the murk with
Shouldn't they do horoscopes
on the nightly news maybe
after sports? I can't see why
we don't pitch this get rich go live
in the woods, pasted, finally do away with
How many poems have I written in order to say the sea
    is haunted
they tell me "piracy is so old-fashioned"
but does that little ad factory
know the story of the submarine
and the slave ship?

the afternoons we've spent
failing to overcome time
parceled into packets via half pints
and little gasps and gropes

Can you do my zipper?
can I have some more juice?
I gave you that ring
because a ring is a vessel
Maybe we'll live forever petting
bell-shaped medusa domes
and bosses everywhere evaporate
and the palace of Versailles
in Tampa, Florida kabooms
and this list will have to be as long as
the catalog of horrors
What does Aristotle say
about sacrificial beauty
at the bottom of the ocean?
I want to spend the rest of my days
as an immortal hydroid
Call me polyp

Idea World

the monuments
are falling the monuments
are being burned down

the world being
already on fire
and the lungs
mucked up with bile

issue out this toxic gas
and we in arrears
hack back

I am fat
on duck and the ground
up bones of wealth
which feeds me

will I die
before my stench
diminishes?

I want to set a leg
of lamb a big

old endless ham
down onto the earth

or to bed
in the branches
of the oldest tree
beyond reach
of bosses & captains

and light myself
into disappearing
dust

Calling Convergence

properly ensconced
begloved I walk
an egret
without regret

a bare branch
appears flimsy
but the strength
of the core
of the whole earth holds it

sinew is courageous
courage is nothing but
the agreement of form &
the material for giving

this song facilitates
the open
dear leader
limits its use

so we launch attacks
against the regime
of ossification

My Froggy Heart

What governs the transformation
of the hailing & entering
of the moonlit future
rich in efficacy of causes, really
real like apples or cylinders
of compressed air for buoyancy
for others beckoned by the tide
where workers cease work
and lay down that vow
endemic to enterprise
every impulse against
what's good for Glencore
for love of that world
in which the ruby never breaks
If only a fool is mesmerized
by what a mouth could cup
then call me a fan
of what flaps about the deck
The bait was so salty, sir
I could not refuse
my mammalian body lacks nuance
Tea time under the coverlet
Carry me away, eelpout

My Friend the Forest

Two jackets in the lake this morn
and 25¢ for a wing

arm in arm with the sod
I cower and veer according

to the density of the swarm
to be quickest among the living-dead

I endeavor
by band and by force

to bring the future into focus
by pecking the rash

which when no longer throbbing
thrives by festering

What's engorged and toss
turning all over?

the optative's white flag
beyond the surround

of its initial transmission
or despite everything

in the hot wind
I carve out a space

to make refrain
glad of a piece

of hanged bacon
so I never leave

the glass-bottomed Mazda
in a green crush of reeds

at so long marina
someone's leaning on the horn

let's "slip crosswise
through the grid-structured surveillance"

a little with the wing now please
and some with the thighs

trees like these
Oh trees like these

California Compliant

walking slowly across the colony

cups on the lawn and a champagne cork

my favorite water storage district

the leaky milk of established fact

who here thinks a woman is soft

who persists in entering

a mismanaged idea of linkage

the star system and hit parade

giving rhythm to the round dance

operational beyond its own syntax

dread-drenched in the backseat

meteorites strike the sky and the abyss

opens in four directions

the morning light never looked so

fourteen kinds of melancholy

and you think the ocean is a drift

they come in such numbers

open your eyes, blue

Sheepskin City

I am given the job of interpreting pings
I am given one hour off leash
to take my picnic to the cherry snow
and ask my mouth to do the contemplating

I squint and imagine
taking a left where
the clover's been
a blue brooch

Across the way
they're turning
errant oak to dust, gone
two blocks of eldest trunk
to save what
the cracking concrete?

Even if I gather all my friends together
and light the diorama with a pearl
There is no spring break for debt

They say the color blue
is an invention of culture
"sky, suede, corn, and midnight"

The light is doing something
on that tree for you Peter

People have dogs
and they walk them

Always Crashing in the Same Car

on solstice eve
bpNichol, black sesame
and Basho, having seen the blood
and the wilting curdled stems
debt loads for graduates
and latin names for trees

when I went to birdtown
when I was young and
spread about the lawn
which glowed in its beginnings
now waning beats the breath

"the universe is ruled by love
and countervalent sorrow"
the union is prior
to anatomic meaning
in actual episodic functioning

you may know these lines by heart
sobbing in a Saab
banking on the closing bell
to have conceded nothing

to contemporary need
did you make it through
the polar night unscathed?

Thinking of a Dream I Had

who among us
will turn back
on rushing water
in the hole where we inn

I don't think it's possible
everybody has theories
mine don't breed with muses
and call that SARS

wept into the car
and into the sofa
spat continuing
to believe care is constancy
until pouring
and poring over my letter
to the dead clock
with my one good
eye streaming

how have you chosen
on this oily earth
to live you can die

of a broken
you know
it is not courage
but ripe deafness

no promise holds
tight to the world
only this one sun
or maybe I should call you
sludge for breakfast

since 1922
Kingfish comforts
where I lose my favorite
jacket with the gold
latch and spark

Do You Perverts Have I.D.?

What's true of facts is true of course
of love & meter, words adapt
and assemble that lack
prehensile police
claw at the mouth
of the trap door
til my ears ring

What do you know
of the natural world?
Troops train to turn
everything shrub
30,000 wolves
empty out onto Club Med

What's a plea if it's too poor
to lay down and gather
smooth rocks in repose

What's the Greek word for
you've got some pollen on your nose
and of the dry grass in the last open plain
whose touch takes place

in the real floral field
the ripe syllogism
of our keeping

I seem to want
as long as
I seem to want

There is no pill
that I know of
but I will demonstrate urge
and need in fine elocution
What attains
fear is the opposite

Our Portrait Exceeds Us

There is a burning star and there is a gift
of choice at least sometimes
once something will come
from the world, it just appears
from nowhere
making event
of the given
heat-guided drives

for public use
for ease of swallowing
honey, fog, and come what may
unsteady in the gravel
unsteady in the sandy murk

I never said
the end I said
credit functions
on the edifice
of the routine
of pillage and extinction
debt swallows the moon

as an ear's for
tonguing the open out
an ear's for breathing
engine of thought
knowing what
listens won't die
but it's hard to hear
it's hard to hear

Horsehair and Roseshirt

a duck is talking
to what remains
of the perennials

a small yellow bud
facilitates the open
I walk into my life

as before
so below

the lone gray wolf
the rare river
otter's return

thumb don't put me
under lift me up

Wabenzi

In bright day
configured
by the credit
bearing chain
an agent aims
to distinguish the intellect
from the imagination
from the standpoint of what
seeks to control it
from flophouse
to chopping block
Hello world hello deed
what lies between
want and need
in guttural gesture
in coated pluming
which republic is this?
which way do the buses point tonight?
Host me in the country
take me to fish ladder
tell me of the ways
of no future and when the line
runs dry when truck

with practicality swerves
"keep your weakness intact"
watch geese tidy crabgrass
and the gull get its hotcake
Embassies are burning
lay those deputies down

Singing from My Little Point

After months of mishearing
thank you for the thought
that all my loving can be bought
I see now clapping
on the backbeat it's
embrace your finitude
as the end of accumulation

Cloak wrapped so tight
it beeps when I cross
the border or dip
a toe in the ocean

Baton to rib
baton to rose quartz
it takes a while for the swelling to recede

I prefer pigs
to drip with milk
to flip and find this
slow unfolding
grips the forearm
rings the lifting torso

Call it decision
call it acrobatic embrace
A full-length portrait
of building urge
The hump in the center
is the earth

Breadwinning for Birds

They pay me to lift
the ball off the bat
touch the slender hand
and slip beneath the taut band

I plant bulbs and mulch the mound
I hone a group of black birds
I do the simplest thing

In unison with the trees
people move as the sun moves
He calls a seagull an eagle
and I agree

Across the pond
they say I *will*
I know this is a problem
for the painter, etc.

Tell me where to go
if they ditch me mid-season
tell me a word
seeks its world

Praise be to the upper lip of decision
praise be to dumb clanking stems

Everything is alive
even you, floral loafer

Water, Skim, and Yolk

Beginning If
Beginning Undying lack

Ask of the flimsy
little thing no wings
how could it come to be

Shoot down satellites
and launch brigades

This little bird
pecks straw
this other
catches fledge

Bold brave fact
flips the boat

You Know It Seems the More We Talk About It

On the cooling board
where the wind slaps my face
like a glove white
on rice in a month of Mondays
like likeness doubles
scars, we have nothing
between gasps
of great need
56 slides against
the physiology of emotion
extract a machine
if it survives
of good functioning

but on the underside
of the speaking box
a coin from the free states
slipped in the slot
so out comes a wall
of sound out comes
fierce rock armed
by lifting gale
by heat seeking heart source

so the chest once tapped
glows again as the moon
is no man and roots
in the breath this edict
bald on the pillar
the waves wash it

I Wanna Be Shipmated

If you call to the hill in the gloaming
the incomplete and T-soaked eye of the police
will peer & drone, but they're not birdlife they're not
seabirds in endless articulated drift
which is the engine of embodied thought
some call mere sentiment don't believe them

The fantasy life of 2am "The Breeze /
My Baby Cries" is not for neighbors
All my guidance enters from behind
is not for neighbors
Does water moan?

I trail my finger along the index to mark bifurcation
and run my hand along the moist redwood ridge
having stared into the balm between bridges
breathing with the night herons and whatever
it is that's chirping up from the flood which is our floor

When I feel a bit on my lip that's how I know
what's coursing and inside abundance
is bright lime and white rush
The hand moves of its own accord

What Gathers Us Here Tonight

I venture out
into the hornless night
bearing no news I hardly
have a mouth

Note the decorative
molding over the breast
the jutting sharp cuts on the nest

Oh how a woman ruins
with excessive fluid
and what binds
donor & gift
host & graft

you wish, you want, you hope
you had no choice

The slippage comes
upon waking
I shut my eyes
and see light

where fundament rips
where counterfact dips

face west in the night indebted
watch cargo make marks across the sky

When I say us
I speak as a member
in the billfold of our feeling

friends go to Michigan
and don't come back

Take My Hand

Snout aground
rooting for tubers
for the sulking kairos
mourning is part of
the youth in their shorts
sprawl across the square
in phones

If you cut a conditional
in half and belief and fear
this picture of division
pits the future against its body

I have no smooth head
over which to run my right
hand but I'm rooting
for him I'm rooting
for every tender thing
for my sister
and for you

Not so much fearless
but contingent
But I repeat myself
but please repeat yourself

In the Craving Night

No debt jubilee
no fiery overcome
I weld & wend
the idea the mind
contains the idea
of the body by cause
of its own envelope

I fail at that game
no judge for size
for Platonic form
How bright in flame
how ripe in hoard
Indeed how much gold
bespoke the rope
we dangle from

What's dead & banking?
What sounds the sea-deep?

In school they'll teach you
to map gridlines & build hedges
to mark this land for grazing

and that land for razing
In school they'll teach you
the world's not made of words
but greet this hole
born of sound
bigger than circumstance
no origins but in
burning arcades
my Nikes alight

Defile that smirking code
let loose of labor
we want the order
of clouds the heart's long-ship
the animated world
of love in her youth
owner of no oval office
A collective wilding
tongues the trunk
the loot's the problem

My Teacup

trees are steaming
ever more vital pliant DINK
I can't see a thing in the sky
I choose George
Stanley over Fear
and Trembling
Tell why you chose
to do this or that
on each occasion
Nothing with hooves
or heels was it?
Excuse me for not thumbing
the abyss, "the goading urgency
of contingent happenings"
how stretchy the membrane
how drunk the ship
breaching the freight
we port with
however it is
I am and come to know
the ruby field of feeling
and isn't a life suddenly
laid in all its excess

of doubt & dualism
gag in the mouth I forget
to give sense to
relations that animate
to be carried among them
you are not an engineer
yet forms persist
so topple the column
any place there's a rope there's
the earth is not enough
I stick my head in it
I lose my coat

I Want to Thank the Wind Blows

Sound of the rain so I know
there's constraint
sound of the train
so I know commerce
has not come to a standstill
now they raise the barrier
now they set it back in place

What coats the bottom
of the surface of the sound
when the swifts come in
when the clerks come home
who will bathe the children
who will bake the bread

when the luff is tight
when the mainsheet
starts the boat underway

whatever you do don't
let the tongue slip
from its moorings

what's that song?
love lift us up where we belong

I ate the pill
and the pill was real

Acknowledgments

Some of these poems previously appeared in the chapbook *Don't Go Home with Your Heart On*, and in the following publications: *Black Box: A Record of the Catastrophe*, *c_L newsletter*, *Compost*, *Cordite Poetry Review*, *Elderly*, *Feminist Formations*, *Lana Turner*, *Landowich*, *Materials*, *New American Writing*, SFMOMA *Open Space*, *P-Queue*, *Poem-A-Day* from the Academy of American Poets, *Poetry*, *Streetnotes*, *The Emerald Tablet*, *The Feralist*. Thanks to the editors for their support.

Gratitude to Lindsey Boldt, Julian Brolaski, Rodney Koeneke, Lauren Levin, Trisha Low, Cynthia Sailers, Cedar Sigo, and Stephanie Young. Thank you to Nightboat Books. And to Brandon Brown for everything.

Alli Warren's most recent published works include *Don't Go Home With Your Heart On* and Poetry Center Book Award winner *Here Come the Warm Jets*. Her writing has been published in many journals and magazines, including *Poetry*, *The Brooklyn Rail*, *Jacket*, and *Rethinking Marxism*. She previously co-curated The (New) Reading Series at 21 Grand, edited *Dreamboat* magazine, and co-edited *The Poetic Labor Project*.

NIGHTBOAT BOOKS

Nightboat Books, a nonprofit organization, seeks to develop audiences for writers whose work resists convention and transcends boundaries. We publish books rich with poignancy, intelligence, and risk. Please visit our website, www.nightboat. org, to learn about our titles and how you can support our future publications.

The following individuals have supported the publication of this book. We thank them for their generosity and commitment to the mission of Nightboat Books:

Elizabeth Motika
Benjamin Taylor

In addition, this book has been made possible, in part, by grants from the National Endowment for the Arts and the New York State Council on the Arts Literature Program.